CHRISTMAS Stories

COLIN S. SMITH

10 Publishing
a division of 10 of those.com

British Library Cataloguing in Publication Data
A record for this book is available from the British Library

ISBN: 978-1-837280-43-8

Designed by Pete Barnsley (CreativeHoot.com)

Printed in ShenZhen, China

Published in association with the literary agency of Wolgemuth & Wilson

10Publishing, a division of 10ofthose.com
Unit C, Tomlinson Road, Leyland, PR25 2DY, England

info@10ofthose.com
www.10ofthose.com

1 3 5 7 10 8 6 4 2

CONTENTS

GABRIEL'S
Story

OF ALL THE ANGELS IN HEAVEN, I was the one who was given the privilege of announcing the coming of Jesus Christ into the world. I can't tell you how many angels there are, but when the apostle John caught a glimpse of us, he reported seeing more than a hundred million angels, and those are just the ones that he saw. Frankly, I've got more important things to do than try to count them, but I suspect that there are at least as many angels as there are people in the world.

People who become fascinated with angels have usually missed the point, which is that we are fascinated with God. The great privilege of my life is to stand in His presence, and to see how God's love flows between the Father, the Son and the Spirit, and from them to us all.

Let me tell you about myself before I get into my story. Did you know that there are only two angels mentioned *by name* in the Bible? One is Michael the archangel, and the other is me—Gabriel. I was chosen as God's messenger, not once, but three times!

I was sent to the prophet Daniel. He had been given a vision, but he didn't understand it, and I was sent to help him make sense of it all.

When I appeared to him, he was so devastated that he fell on the ground trembling, and it took him days to recover.

My second assignment was to visit Zechariah, a priest serving in the temple of God. My mission was to announce the birth of John the Baptist, and when I appeared to Zechariah, he too was gripped with fear. I told him what God would do, but he didn't believe it.

Well, you can't have spiritual leaders spreading unbelief, so the gift of speech was taken from him until the boy was born. And when his speech returned, he used it to praise and worship God.

My visits to Daniel and Zechariah had clearly terrified them, so when I was sent on a mission to a country girl in her early teens, my first instinct was to wonder, *Am I the right one for the job?*

"There is a young woman to whom you must give this message," I was told. "It is the most important announcement I have ever made. The future of the world hangs on it."

When I heard the message, I was the one who couldn't speak. I could hardly take it in. The truth is, I still can't.

I took down the details and off I went, not to Jerusalem, not to the temple, not to a daughter of Caiaphas the High Priest, but to a peasant girl in a despised little town called Nazareth. Why she was chosen, I cannot say. All I can tell you is that He has the right to choose.

A Meeting with Mary

The young woman's name was Mary, and she was a virgin, pledged to be married to a man called Joseph. Their marriage was planned, but it had not yet taken place.

When I appeared, I gave her my warmest greeting. "Greetings, you who are highly favored! The Lord is with you."

I don't know who was more afraid—she of what was happening, or me of how she might respond. What if she screamed and ran away? But it was obvious to me that she was a woman of faith, and she seemed to sense that I had come as a messenger from the Lord.

Seeing how much she was troubled I said, "Don't be afraid, Mary, you have found *favor* with God." The word favor means "grace." "You have been graced by God"—that's what I told her.

Then I gave her the message: "You will be with child, and give birth to a Son," I said. "And you are to give Him the name Jesus. He will be great and will be called the Son of the Most High. The Lord God will give Him the throne of his father David, and He will reign over the house of Jacob forever; His kingdom will never end."

I paused and wondered what she would say. It seemed as if time stood still, just as it does in eternity. Then she spoke: "How will this be," she asked, "since I am a virgin?"

She hadn't grasped what I was saying. She thought I meant that she and her future husband would have a son who would turn out to be one of the great figures of human history.

So I tried to explain. It wasn't easy to find words to express the greatest mystery your world has ever known. "The Holy Spirit will come upon you," I said. "And the power of the Most High will overshadow you. So the Holy One to be born will be called the Son of God."

How God could take human form and be born into the world as a helpless baby is beyond what even angels can understand. All I can tell you is what I told Mary, "Nothing is impossible with God."

God works through people who freely and gladly obey Him. He has a way of drawing our wills like a lover, but He does not force His will on anyone.

So Mary had a choice to make, and I trembled as I waited to hear what she would say. Then she spoke. "I am the Lord's servant," she said. "Let it be to me as you have said."

JESUS

And so it was that nine months later, Jesus was born. A whole company of my colleagues appeared in the sky that night, praising God and announcing the good news to men and women.

We marveled as we watched His life. He was everything God intended a person to be, and His ministry brought more good to the world in three years than anything else we had seen in all of human history. That's why we could hardly believe it when we saw what happened next: You crucified him.

I'll never forget that day. We watched in horror as He was scourged and bound and led away. We waited for Him to call on us, but He never did. When He was nailed to the cross, we said to the Father: "Please, let us go and save Him!" But He held us back.

Human beings have done some terrible things, but this was the worst of all. God's judgment had to fall that day. And it did. But to our complete astonishment, it fell on Jesus! He absorbed God's judgment in His own body, on *your* behalf. He gave Himself as the sacrifice for *your* sins.

When He died, heaven fell silent.

It wasn't until the third day that we understood what God was doing. I will never forget that glorious morning. The corpse of

Jesus that had been laid in a sealed tomb was animated with His life. His human body was transformed and adapted for eternity.

When the women came to the tomb looking for His body, another angel was sent to tell them, "He is risen!" After that, He appeared to His disciples many times, and then he ascended into heaven. You can imagine our joy in receiving Him back.

But your joy should be even greater than ours. Jesus didn't die for angels. It wasn't the nature of angels that He assumed when He came into the world. God became a man. He died and rose again for people like you.

GOD BECAME A MAN. HE DIED AND ROSE AGAIN FOR PEOPLE LIKE YOU.

There's a *man* in heaven, and His name is Jesus. He is there for you. He is the pioneer—the first of many men and women who will rejoice forever in the presence of God for all eternity.

All the talk up here now is about the day of His second coming. I will be with Him then, along with all who love and trust Him, and I hope that you will be there too.

A CELEBRATION IN HEAVEN

There are some things known to me that are hidden from you, and there are other things known to you that are hidden from me. Do you have any idea how privileged you are to have your sins forgiven, to be reconciled to God, and to have God's Spirit living in you?

I have never been lost, so I cannot know the joy of being found. I have never sinned, so I cannot imagine what it is like to be forgiven. The intimacy with God that is possible for you is staggering to me. You can experience the love of God in ways that I can never know.

But there are other things known to me that are hidden from you. You cannot imagine heaven or hell. You cannot begin to picture what Jesus has saved you from or what He has saved you for.

What's staggering to me is that so many humans give such little thought to their eternal future, living as if this fleeting world was everything, totally unaware of the eternity that is just beyond your line of sight.

But I have to tell you that every time a sinner repents, there is a great celebration in heaven. God is for you and however far you may be from Him today, He wants you back.

That is why Jesus Christ came into the world. He came to seek and to save the lost, and to give His life as a ransom for many. Believe in Him and you will not be disappointed. Follow Him and He will lead you into greater joy than you have ever known.

PRAYER

Father, thank you for sending Jesus into the world for us.

And thank you for reminding us today that Jesus is the greatest joy of heaven.

May He be our greatest joy too! Amen.

MARY'S *Story*

THE DAY THAT CHANGED MY LIFE FOREVER started out like any other. I had been following my usual routine of chores, when suddenly, I felt the presence of someone else beside me.

Slowly I looked up and there he was. God sent an angel to me and when he appeared, I have to tell you, I was terrified. My heart was pounding, my knees were shaking, and if I hadn't sat down, I would probably have passed out.

When God draws near, there is something in all of us that assumes the worst. We feel safe with God at a distance, and we fear that if He gets too close we might be in trouble.

But the angel said to me, "Do not be afraid, Mary, you have found favor with God." *Favor* simply means "grace," God's kindness—not deserved, but freely given, and God was showing grace to me.

Seeing God's Power

What the angel said next was absolutely stunning, "Mary, you will be with child and you will give birth to a son. You are to give Him the name Jesus. He will be great and will be called the Son of the Most High. The Lord will give Him the throne of His father David, and He will reign over the house of Jacob forever."

A child? How could that be? I was a virgin.

A child of mine on the throne of David? How could that ever happen? I come from an ordinary family. We were certainly not the kind who lived in palaces or socialized with kings.

A child who would reign forever? Nothing in this world lasts forever, so how could that possibly be?

But most baffling of all, the angel said that the child to be born would be "the Son of the Most High." How could any child of mine ever be the Son of God?

The angel had the answer: "The Holy Spirit will come upon you, and the power of the Most High will overshadow you. So, the Holy One to be born will be called the Son of God."

I still marvel at the mystery of what God accomplished. He caused a new life to be conceived in my womb, and that life was the life of His own Son. It was in and through me that God took flesh and was born into the world just like any other helpless baby.

There was more. The angel told me that my older cousin Elizabeth, who had longed for a child of her own for many years, had now conceived and was already in the sixth month of her pregnancy. "Nothing will be impossible with God," the angel said.

> SO, THE HOLY ONE TO BE BORN WILL BE CALLED THE SON OF GOD."

I hardly knew how to respond. What was promised to me was beyond my understanding, and what would be required of me I dared not even think. And yet, at that very moment, I knew that God's Spirit was with me, and that He would give me all that I would ever need.

"Let it be to me according to your word," I said.
And then the angel was gone.

ELIZABETH AND JOSEPH

I decided to go and stay with my cousin Elizabeth, and when I arrived at her house, we were both overwhelmed with joy. "Who would have imagined that after all these years of longing for a child, God would bless you with this marvelous gift," I said.

Elizabeth looked radiant as she stood in the doorway with the palms of her hands gently placed over the child she was carrying. "When the sound of your greeting came to my ears, the baby in my womb leapt for joy," she said. That meant that three of us were rejoicing, and there was no doubt in my mind that God in heaven was rejoicing too.

Then God's Spirit came on Elizabeth, and in a loud voice she said to me: "Blessed are you among women, and blessed is the child that you will bear."

How did she know that I was expecting? I had not yet said anything to Elizabeth about the child I was carrying. The only way she could have known was that *God* had revealed this to her!

Then Elizabeth said some words I will never forget: "Blessed is she who believed that there would be a fulfillment of what was spoken to her from the Lord."

I had already believed that God's promise would be fulfilled. But Elizabeth came alongside me and strengthened my faith: "Mary, the promise *will* be fulfilled. What God has said will be accomplished."

I couldn't contain the joy that I felt. The Son of God was coming into the world and I was carrying His life within me. My whole being was filled with praise that burst out and overflowed in words that were given to me:

"My soul magnifies the Lord,
and my spirit rejoices in God my Savior,
for he has looked on the humble estate of his servant.
For behold, from now on all generations will call me blessed;
for he who is mighty has done great things for me, and
holy is his name."

Throughout my time with Elizabeth, I kept wondering what Joseph would do. We were pledged to be married, and both of us had been eagerly awaiting our wedding day. Joseph was a good man and I knew that he loved me deeply, but I could hardly expect him to grasp what God was doing. I thought that he might divorce me, and if this was the price of the calling God had laid on my life, I was ready to pay it.

"DO NOT FEAR TO TAKE MARY AS YOUR WIFE."

So you can imagine my joy when Joseph told me that an angel had spoken to him in a dream. "Do not fear to take Mary as your wife," the angel had said, "for that which is conceived in her is from the Holy Spirit. And there's something else," Joseph said. "I am to give Him the name Jesus."

What the angel said to Joseph matched exactly with what the angel had said to me. It was another confirmation of God's promise.

Bethlehem and the Shepherd

Shortly before the child was born, a decree was issued requiring everyone in the country to register in the place where they were born. That meant that I had to travel with Joseph to Bethlehem.

The little town only had one inn, and when we arrived it was already full. So we found a place of shelter with the animals and it was there that Jesus was born.

It seemed strange being there, just the three of us. The greatest miracle the world had ever known lying in my arms and, as far as I was aware, Joseph and I were the only ones who knew what God had done.

But that soon changed. Before the night of His birth had passed, I heard the sound of some men coming toward our shelter. One of them told us that an angel had appeared to them, and that they had all been filled with fear. I smiled, knowing exactly what they had felt.

Then another stepped forward. "But the angel told us not to be afraid, and then he said, "I bring you good news of great joy that will be for all the people. For unto you is born this day in the city of David, a Savior, who is Christ the Lord."

A Savior! The angel had told Joseph, "You shall call His name Jesus for He will save His people from their sins."

God had spoken to these shepherds and I listened intently to what they said. They confirmed again that Jesus is the promised Messiah, that His birth is good news for all people, and that He is the Lord of all.

Everything they said matched what had been revealed to Joseph and to me. So I stored all these things in my memory and pondered them in my heart.

The Temple and the Cross

Some weeks after Jesus was born, we went to the temple in Jerusalem to offer a sacrifice and to present Jesus before the

Lord. While we were there, an old man came up to us and asked if he could hold the child in his arms. He told us that all his life, he had been waiting for the promised Messiah and that God had told him he would see the child before he died.

Taking Jesus in his arms, the old man blessed Him, and then he pronounced a blessing over Joseph and me.

Speaking words that were clearly given to him by the Holy Spirit, he said, "This child is appointed for a sign that is opposed." And then, looking directly at me with sadness and compassion in his eyes, he said, "And a sword will pierce through your soul also."

> JESUS IS THE PROMISED MESSIAH, THAT HIS BIRTH IS GOOD NEWS FOR ALL PEOPLE, AND THAT HE IS THE LORD OF ALL.

The child opposed? And a sword piercing me?

These were words that I often pondered, and they painfully proved to be true for Jesus and for me. He came to His own, but His own did not receive Him. Plots against Him began early in His ministry, and in the end they hung Him on a cross.

> ON THE THIRD DAY, HE ROSE FROM THE GRAVE. HE ASCENDED INTO HEAVEN AND OPENED ITS GATES FOR ME AND FOR ALL WHO TRUST IN HIM.

I was there. And when the nails pierced His hands, it was as if a sword pierced my soul, just as the old man had said. But the agony I suffered was nothing in comparison to the pain He endured. Jesus bore our sins when He suffered on the cross. He took them on Himself so that we might be forgiven, saved, and at peace with God.

I was overwhelmed with sorrow when Jesus died. But thank God it didn't end there. On the third day, He rose from the grave. He ascended into heaven and opened its gates for me and for all who trust in Him.

Prayer

Father, thank you for your grace that is ours in the coming of Jesus Christ.

Thank you that He came into the world to save and rescue. Help me put my faith and trust in Him.

Help us to believe that nothing is impossible with you!

Amen.

JOSEPH'S *Story*

I HAD A FRONT-ROW SEAT for the greatest event that has ever happened in the history of the world. I was pledged to be married to Mary. What I didn't know was that she had been chosen by God to give birth to the Savior of the world. The first thing that you need to know about Mary's child is that His birth had absolutely nothing whatsoever to do with me. We knew that the union of a man and a woman was sacred, and that it was kept for marriage. I had kept myself for Mary, and Mary had kept herself for me. That's why I was completely devastated when she came to me with the news that shattered our world.

I can't imagine how hard it was for her to tell me her story. She said something about an angel, but all I can remember is that she said the word "pregnant." I was distraught. My dream of marriage had become a nightmare.

There was no way I could go forward with the marriage. How could I do that with someone who had betrayed my trust? I know that no woman has a child without a man. At least that's how I saw it at the time. I still loved her and I didn't want to hurt her, but going ahead with the marriage was not an option for me.

Mary told me she thought the best thing would be for her to go away and stay with her cousin Elizabeth, who lived in Judea. My world was shattered. One minute I was on the brink of marriage to the woman I loved, the next I was sitting in my carpenter's shop all alone.

HOW GOD SPOKE TO ME

Then one night I had an experience that was unlike anything that had ever happened to me before. An angel of the Lord appeared to me in a dream and said, "Joseph, son of David, do not fear to take Mary as your wife, because that which is conceived in her is from the Holy Spirit. She will bear a son, and you shall call His name Jesus, for He will save His people from their sins."

> "A VIRGIN WILL CONCEIVE AND WILL GIVE BIRTH TO A SON."

When I woke up, a verse of Scripture I had learned in the synagogue came back to my mind. God had promised that He would send the Messiah. And when Isaiah spoke of how this deliverer would be born into the world, he said, "A *virgin* will conceive and will give birth to a son."

A virgin! But there was more. Isaiah said that the child born of a virgin would be *Immanuel*, which means God with us. From earliest times, God had promised to send a deliverer into the world. Could it be that God was about to fulfill His ancient promise? Slowly, but surely, I began to believe.

I knew what I had to do and I headed south to Judea, hardly able to wait to take my beloved Mary in my arms and tell her what had happened.

"I have something to tell you," I said. "An angel of the Lord appeared to me in a dream." Mary smiled, and I sensed that she was not entirely surprised.

"What did he say?" she asked.

"Three things," I said. "First, he told me not to be afraid. Then he said that what is conceived in you is from the Holy Spirit..."

Mary could hardly contain her joy. "Joseph, I tried to tell you before that an angel appeared to me! And what he told me is exactly what he said to you! The angel told me not to be afraid, and then he said that I would have a son. When I asked how this could be since I was a virgin, he told me it that this would be the work of the Holy Spirit. "The Holy Spirit will come upon you and the power of the Most High will overshadow you."

We looked at each other, stunned by what had been revealed to us.

"There's something else," I said, eager to complete my story. "The angel gave me the child's name."

"Tell me," Mary said, her eyes wide with anticipation.

"The angel told me to call him..." I paused, and before I could finish, Mary said, "Jesus!"

"How did you know that?" I asked.

"The angel told me too," she said.

We fell into each other's arms, overwhelmed by the kindness of God who had brought us together by giving us the same amazing revelation. God was sending His Son into the world and our little lives had been caught up in the sweep of His saving purpose. The more I thought about it, the more staggering it seemed.

In glad obedience to what God had told me, I took Mary home as my wife, but I had no union with her until after the child was born.

OUR JOURNEY TO BETHLEHEM

Some months later, a messenger arrived in town with news from Rome of a new government initiative. The entire population was ordered to return to their town of family origin to register for a census. Can you imagine it? It seemed as if everyone was on the move.

The roads were in chaos—families with carts and animals moving in every direction.

Mary was nearly due, but when the Romans gave orders there were no exceptions. So I saddled up the donkey and the two of us headed south on the road to my hometown of Bethlehem.

Only later did I realize that even this was in the plan of God. The prophet Micah had said that the Messiah would come out of Bethlehem. And God put it into the mind of a Roman emperor to issue an order that required us to go to Bethlehem when Jesus was about to be born. Amazing!

Bethlehem was overcrowded when we arrived and there was no room for us at the inn. So we took shelter with the animals.

Gathering some straw, I made a bed for Mary, and that was where Jesus was born.

I cannot describe the joy of that moment to you. I was the first one to touch the gift of God. My hands brought Him into the world, and I was the first to hold Him in my arms.

The Wise Men

After Jesus was born, I found a house and we settled into a regular routine in Bethlehem. But one night, our quiet lives were interrupted when three men arrived saying that they were kings and that they had come to see Jesus. These kings were from the east. They were Gentiles, and God had spoken to them through a star that had led them on a long journey to Bethlehem. When they saw Jesus, these kings fell down on their faces and worshipped Him. Then they opened the gifts they had brought for Him—gold, frankincense and myrrh.

I still laugh when I think about their visit. These kings had so much, and we had so little. God brought the richest and the poorest together around Jesus, and we were united as one as we worshipped Him.

Traveling Again

When the kings left us, an angel of the Lord spoke to me in another dream. "Rise," he said. "Take the child and

His mother, and flee to Egypt, for Herod is about to search for the child, to destroy Him."

Destroy Him? Why would Herod want to destroy the Savior of the world? Why, when kings from other nations worshipped Him, would our king want to kill Him?

It made no sense to me, but God had spoken, and I knew that we had to obey. So we packed up what we could, slipped out of Bethlehem under the cover of darkness, and I took Jesus and His mother to Egypt, the place from which God had once delivered our people. How strange that the place where our forefathers were once slaves became the place in which Jesus should find safety.

Sometime later we heard that Herod had died. It was safe to return home and when we did, we settled in Nazareth where I continued my work as a carpenter.

There's so much more to my story, but I have to stop here for now. One more thing before I do: If you find it hard to believe in the virgin birth, how do you think it was for me? Nobody found it harder to believe than I did. But I can tell you that He was born of a virgin.

And here's why that matters: Being born of a virgin, Jesus is unlike any other person who has ever lived, and He is able to do for you what no one else can do.

PRAYER

Father, thank you for sending your Son, Jesus, into the world.

We cannot fully grasp all that you have told us about His birth, but we fall to our knees in wonder, as we consider His greatness and glory!

Amen.

SIMEON'S
Story

I WASN'T IN BETHLEHEM. I didn't see the angels. And I didn't visit the inn. But I did hold Jesus in my arms forty days after he was born.

I was just an ordinary person living in Jerusalem, except for one thing. Some years earlier, God had revealed to me that I would see the Messiah before I died.

Don't ask me to explain that. All I can tell you is that after it was revealed to me, I knew beyond a shadow of a doubt that I would not die until I had seen the deliverer for whom the whole world had been waiting.

By the way, it is an interesting experience knowing that you will live to see a future event. There were times when I was quite ill and people wondered if I would recover. But I was never in doubt. God had promised that I would see his Christ. So I was immortal until He came!

I sometimes wondered how I would know Him when I saw Him, but somehow deep down inside, I just knew that I would.

The Day it Happened

Well now, let me tell you about the day it happened. It seemed like my whole life was a preparation for that day.

The strange thing is that it was a day like any other. I was going about my usual business, when I felt this inner compulsion to go to the temple. God did not usually speak to me this way, but it was like a voice in my head saying to me, "Simeon, go to the temple."

My first thought was: *I'll go on my way home after work,* but I knew that would be disobedience. All I can say is that I knew that I had to leave what I was doing and go to the temple right away. And I'm so glad I did!

The temple court was a constant hive of activity—traders selling animals, priests offering sacrifices, people confessing their sins, and parents presenting their firstborn sons to the Lord.

When I arrived, a young couple was standing before the priest with their baby. The priest had no idea who He was. But as I watched, I knew that He was the One.

Don't ask me how I knew it. I cannot tell you except to say that the Holy Spirit of God revealed this to me. I was never more sure of anything in all my life. This child was the One the whole world had been waiting for.

I WAS NEVER MORE SURE OF ANYTHING IN ALL MY LIFE. THIS CHILD WAS THE ONE THE WHOLE WORLD HAD BEEN WAITING FOR.

Nobody worked it out on their own. Angels told the shepherds, the wise men were led by a star, and the Holy Spirit revealed it to me.

The evidence that Jesus is the Christ is there for all who seek Him, but it is God who opens your eyes to the truth.

The Words That Were Given to Me

I walked up to the family and stood with the little crowd that had gathered around to watch what was going on.

And that was when it happened. I knew God was giving me words that had to be spoken at that moment. So I tapped Joseph on the arm. I told him that God had given me something to say, and asked if I could hold the child.

"SOVEREIGN LORD, MY EYES HAVE SEEN YOUR SALVATION WHICH YOU PREPARED IN THE SIGHT OF ALL PEOPLE."

He seemed rather surprised, me a stranger and not even a priest, but he agreed, and I found myself holding the child in my arms.

Then the words came. I was speaking but I knew that the words I spoke were given to me. I can only say that I spoke from God as I was carried along by the Holy Spirit.

Holding the child in my arms, I declared, "Sovereign Lord, my eyes have seen your salvation which you prepared in the sight of all people. A light for revelation to the Gentiles and for glory to your people Israel."

I was about to hand the baby back to Mary, but then more words came to me. Like a wind blowing into my body, these words forced their weight upon me, and I had to speak them out:

"This child is destined to cause the falling and rising of many in Israel." The words seemed strange to me. I could understand "rising" but why "falling"?

The words kept coming. "He will be a sign that is spoken against, so that the thoughts of many hearts will be revealed." I could hardly believe the words I was speaking. How could this promised child be spoken against?

I looked at Mary. There was a beauty in her eyes that radiated from the depth of her soul. And as I looked at her, I heard myself say, "And a sword will pierce your own soul too."

We all stood rooted to the spot.

What could this possibly mean?

The Words That Were Given to Anna

Just then, an old lady arrived. Her name was Anna, and she was known to be a woman of prayer. She gave herself to worship and fasting, and people who went to the temple regularly knew that you could count on finding her there!

I had just spoken about the pain that would come to Mary's soul, when Anna walked up, and began praising God. It was the strangest thing. I was still trying to take in how Jesus could be spoken against, and how Mary's soul would be torn in two, and right then God gave Anna words of praise and thanksgiving that came pouring out of her.

If the child would be spoken against, and Mary's soul would be pierced, why was God giving Anna words of thanksgiving?

I think she had grasped what I now understand. Jesus would deliver us at the cost of indescribable pain.

I recalled to mind an old prophecy that said that the God's chosen One would be wounded for our transgressions and bruised for our iniquities. And that the punishment that he faced would bring us peace.

You Won't Have to Wait

That reminds me of the last thing I wanted to tell you: When I held Him in my arms, I knew that I could die in peace.

People had all kinds of hopes and dreams about what the Lord's Christ would do, but there was no doubt in my mind which was the biggest.

He made death safe for all His people. I'm not saying that He made it painless or desirable. It is still our great enemy, but He has made it safe.

He made death safe for all His people.

I knew that my death would be a release from this old, tired body. And that is what happened a short time later.

When I died, I entered eternity. It was like feeling drowsy and barely awake. I don't know how long I was there, time isn't the same on the other side. But I know when it ended. Who could forget that day!

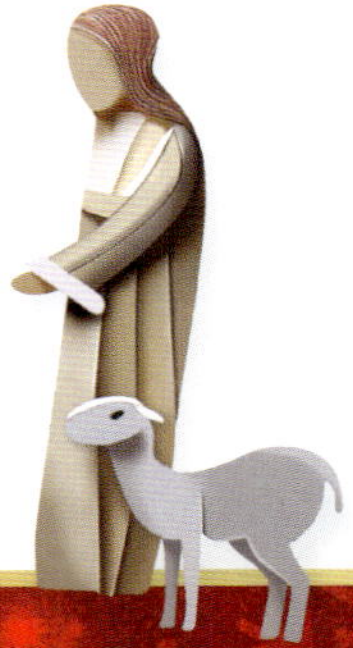

Suddenly everything shook. We saw Jesus. He said, "Come up here," and immediately we found ourselves with Him, entering the presence of God without fear and with overwhelming joy.

THE BLIND RECEIVED SIGHT, THE LAME WALKED, THE DEAD WERE RAISED, AND GOOD NEWS WAS PREACHED TO THE POOR.

The good news for you is that you won't have to wait. When you die your soul will go immediately into the presence of the Lord. To be away from the body is to be at home with the Lord. And this is better by far.

I have been here for more than 2,000 years, though no one is counting. And, of course, I found out how my prophecy was fulfilled.

At the age of 30, Jesus began His ministry. God's glory was revealed—the blind received sight, the lame walked, the dead were raised, and good news was preached to the poor.

But as the Holy Spirit revealed to me, people spoke against Him, they plotted against Him, and in the end they nailed Him to a cross. Jesus died, but on the third day He rose again. He lives forever and gives everlasting life to all who believe in Him.

It turns out that His coming was indeed for the falling and rising of many. There is a sense in which every person who has ever lived will either fall or rise because of Him. He is like a great rock. If you stumble over Him in unbelief, He will bring you down. But if you stand on Him in faith, He will lift you up.

Prayer

Father, thank you that Jesus delivered us from our sins through His suffering on the cross.

You sent Him into the world for the falling or rising of every person.

Help us to take hold of Him by faith and be lifted up!

Amen.

HEROD'S
Story

I AM PROBABLY THE MOST UNDER-APPRECIATED LEADER in history. I've always felt that, and I guess I always will. Most people don't even know about the great achievements of my life. I find that extraordinary. How can it be that so much of what I did counts for so little today?

How I Came to Power

Let me tell you about myself. "Herod" was a common enough name in my time, but I was known as "Herod the Great", and my title was well deserved.

The land of the Jews had been in chaos for years—wars, assassinations, and feuds—the whole thing was a mess. Then, the Roman Empire rose. Rome wanted stability, and that was my door of opportunity.

Caesar Augustus put me in charge of the whole area of Judea and beyond.

I was the king of the Jews. I reigned for more than 30 years and throughout that time there was peace and stability.

Of course it took a while to establish order. The first thing I had to do was to sort out the squabbling among the religious leaders. It is amazing how often trouble begins with religious extremists.

Well here's what I did: There were 72 priests in a ruling group called the Sanhedrin. I eliminated 45 of them, and that helped the others to stay focused.

My Legacy and Achievements

The city of Jerusalem was transformed under my leadership. I loved architecture, and I liked to build on a grand scale.

You have to understand that the temple was the single most important building in Jerusalem. The original had been magnificent, but the temple in my day looked rather shabby. So I decided that I would be the one to make it great again. It would be known as *Herod's temple*. It would win the hearts of the people, and it would stand out as one of the lasting wonders of the world.

During my reign, I created more jobs and put up more buildings than any other king. I was known as "Herod the Great" because I brought greater peace and stability than any of my predecessors. You would think that with all my achievements, I would be the most admired king in history. But no, I've never received the credit I deserve.

A lot of it had to do with race. You see, I was an Edomite—an Arab by race, a Jew by religion, and a Roman by sympathy. I was feared by all and loved by none.

The Story of Jesus' Birth

Jerusalem is a big city, but I had good systems in place to keep my finger on the pulse. Information is power, and I made sure that I had plenty of it.

The first I knew about the birth of Jesus was when some foreign kings arrived in Jerusalem, pedaling a story about how they had followed a star, and were looking for a child who was the King of the Jews.

Well, that was *my* title, and I didn't take kindly to the thought of a rival king. I wasn't alone. Our history had been plagued by self-proclaimed "Messiahs" rising up, gaining a following, and causing no end of trouble. No one in Jerusalem wanted to go back to that again.

I could see that trouble was brewing, and I was determined to deal with it decisively. My first move was to call together the chief priests and the teachers of the law. "Where will the Messiah be born?" I asked them.

"In Bethlehem in Judea," they said. And then they gave me chapter and verse. Apparently, Micah had talked about this 800 years beforehand, "But you, Bethlehem, in the land of Judah, are by no means least among the rulers of Judah; for out of you will come a ruler who will be the shepherd of my people Israel."

So we had a location. The next question was to get a fix on the time. So I invited the foreign kings over to the palace, and told them that I had heard about the birth of a royal child. "If the Messiah has been born," I said, "I also want to worship Him. And besides, if the Messiah has come, He will have enemies. I can protect Him. But I need to find Him before His enemies do."

I told the kings to continue their search for the child and to report to me as soon as they found him. Then, as they were leaving, I said, "Oh, by the way—when did this star that you talked about first appear?"

"It's been nearly two years since we first saw it," they said. And with that they were gone, leaving me with the information I really wanted. Two years! Now I had a place and a time. We were looking for a male child under the age of two in the town of Bethlehem.

I waited for the kings to report back to me, but they never returned. I had been double-crossed, and that made me mad. So I asked for an estimate of the number of boys in Bethlehem under the age of two.

It was a small town, and I was told that it would likely be about a dozen, maybe twenty, or thirty at the most.

I called in my agents and told them there was a potential threat to national security—a child under the age of two in Bethlehem. They looked at me in disbelief. But I dispatched them to deal with the problem, which they did with their usual efficiency.

And shortly after that… I died. That was more than 2,000 years ago, so I've had a lot of time to think.

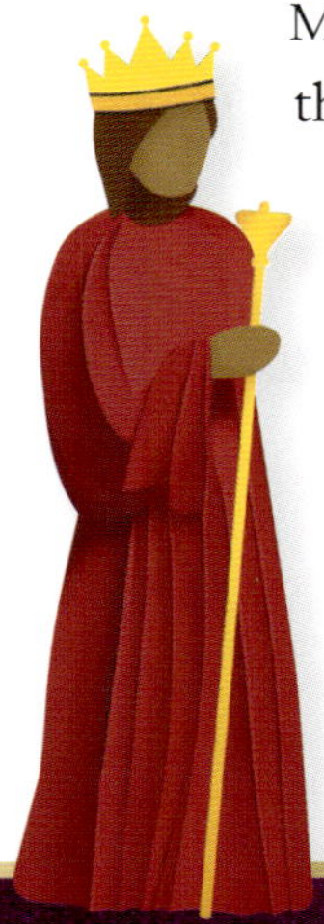

My information down here is rather sketchy, but I've been told that the child was taken by His parents to Egypt and survived. I've heard that thirty years later He began a public ministry, and that my people worked with the Pharisees to do what I had tried to accomplish earlier. I'm told that, in the end, He was crucified. Rumor has it that He rose from the dead, though no one down here believes it.

TRUE GREATNESS

Someone told me that before He was born, an angel appeared to His mother, and said "He will be great." That bothers me, because that was supposed to be my destiny. You know, "Herod the Great!"

The frustrating thing is that no one thinks that what I accomplished is great. I died before my work on the temple was finished and shortly after it was completed, the Romans razed it to the ground. They didn't leave one stone on top of another. So much for my legacy to the world!

The one thing I am remembered for is my antagonism toward Jesus, and today I live with the guilt of my sins in a world of anger, frustration and regret. Every day these things consume me, and I can find no relief from them.

By the way, I've been told that all of the children I murdered in Bethlehem are with safely with Jesus in heaven, and that the full potential of each of their lives is being realized.

I've also heard that heaven is filled with a vast company of people and that many more are on their way. But I will not be among them. I am like a person who stands in the rain, outside a large house, looking through the window as the guests enjoy a party inside.

There was a time when I could have welcomed Jesus, and worshipped Him with the wise men, but I made a different choice. I see now that in trying to rid the world of Jesus, I was fighting against God. I still am, and now I can't stop. That's my story. It's too late for me now. But it's not too late for you.

PRAYER

Father, thank you for the good news that Jesus is the King. Thank you that it is not too late for me to receive Him, by faith, as my king, and live the rest of my life, and all eternity, in the blessing of His kingdom.

Amen.

The true light, which gives light to everyone, was coming into the world. He was in the world, and the world was made through him, yet the world did not know him. He came to his own, and his own people did not receive him. But to all who did receive him, who believed in his name, he gave the right to become children of God, who were born, not of blood nor of the will of the flesh nor of the will of man, but of God. And the Word became flesh and dwelt among us, and we have seen his glory, glory as of the only Son from the Father, full of grace and truth.

JOHN 1:9-14